My inner me

Rabinder Bradley

BookLeaf
Publishing

India | USA | UK

Presentation by *BookLeaf Publishing*

Web: www.bookleafpub.com

E-mail: info@bookleafpub.com

ISBN: 9789358737066

First edition 2023

I want to dedicate this book to my family who are no more but who live in my heart until I die...

ACKNOWLEDGEMENT

I want to thank my friends, family and pets for giving me space to be me. I want to especially thank my sister, my friend, my mentor...who makes mundane life magical!!!

PREFACE

I am writing this book because my life has had so many changes that if I don't publish my journey of poems, I will forget where I came from and the struggles I faced through tough times. On a serious note, I am writing it, so that I can give courage and hope to others like me who face challenges every day but can't find a way forward. I want them to process their emotions through words, write to heal, write to understand, write to get out of yourself and create...
Over time, I have tried unsuccessfully to get these published but it was amateurish. I published a Xmas calendar for myself, and I created a webpage for myself. So, now that my friend has encouraged me, I hope it is worth the effort and it makes a difference to at least one more person's life!

Live and die

Laughter and cries that's what it is
I know it's true, I have lived it through

Then why is it I get so bad
Raging emotions make me mad
So mad that they take over my head

I hurt inside,
Outside...
and my anger
hurts everyone all around...
I feel helpless like a bee
trapped inside a spider's web

Why do I forget?
Who I am?
The joy I brought to
all my friends
Where has the laughter hidden away?
Why can't I call it back to stay?

I am born the part of that
One source
I will die a part of that
One source

What is the lesson I must learn?

That I chose this life to live
and to experience
Once again
with laughter and cries till I die...

Encyclopaedia

We dream, we wish,
We play and make a happy dish
That explodes with sparkles
Pink and blue
Some silver glittery glue

Makes everyone fall in love
Casts a spell to make them feel good
And fly off to encyclopaedia land
Where all the humans have turned into words

And I am Ms. Encyclopaedia
We are playing the hangman
1, 2, 3 and off we go
To the world of fancy fantasy....

Love

Love is hugging and it's bugging
Love is sharing and it's caring
Love is growing and it's daring

It's hugging and kissing
above all its missing
It's looking after
with a heart full of fun and laughter
It's a heart swelled with pride
with the love that's inside
So where does it wander when you get sad?
Is it linked to someone or something or is it just
oxytocin within?
Is it part of our life's memories?

So, let's always promise to make lovely
memories
To take a deep breath and
make way for the smog of anger, hate et al
And welcome fresh fruit of love
Cooked with vegetables of caring
And served on a bed of thoughtfulness
With sweet pudding of kindness
To make the lovely dish of Life

Words

They make me high,
Fly, twirl and float

Like an invincible king
They entice, inspire
Draw me back into the worldly quagmire

What do I say
How do I use
These 'word' knights, bishops and king
Am I their queen?

So be it
That's who I will be
The queen bee who rules
With her wordy army

I command thee words
To be quiet
And just let me be
For sleep beckons
Into my other world of dreams...

Ambition

Ambition- for some it is trampling others
I am great coz others are rubbish

Ambition- for some it is being the best
I am great coz I do lots well

Ambition- for some it is enabling others
I am great coz I let all around me be happy and
great

Ambition- for some it is playing both sides
Schmoozing, kissing backsides

Ambition- for some it is manipulating,
persuasion and control
I am great coz I will make you do what I want

Why do we let this Ambition
Make monsters of us?
Why?

Feeling low

Feeling mad
Feeling sad
Can't get these feelings out of my head

Why do I feel?
Why do I get caught in other people's act?
It affects me so
It hurts me bad
Why can't I just let it go?

Steps

BIG steps
COURAGE
Little steps
Effort

Where has the smile gone?

Where did it go?
In its stead, it left tears
Which don't ever seem to go

Millions of years ago
It was always there in its full glow
It was hard, it was tough
But never could it seem to snuff
This RADIANT JOY - to enjoy the moon, the
sunrise...

Do I need a change of scene?
This perfect measured world
isn't for me
I need the chaos, I need heart
I need cares and the dares
of all things familiar

I need to fly far far away
to the land full of warm
sunshine of love

To family?
To hugs and kisses

To food and rest
To chat and a laugh
To brothers, sisters, uncles and aunts

or to the sandy shores of Seychelles, or
Caribbean...
To snorkel in the sea
And trapeze in my water skis
To relax and unwind
With my own kind

Will it return soon?
Like the new moon?
Growing gently each day...
or is it eclipsed by PLANET BLUE
that ain't budging nowhere...

The Choice is hard
The Choice is key
To unfold this mystery

Wish it was easy, wish it was clear
Wish I had the courage to bear
Consequences I contemplate...

Live wire

On high octane Buzzzzzzz
The mind is in overdrive
It's computing and processing
Thinking, planning, analysing

And the deciding HOW Do I say it
And not let my thoughts stray
Ahead of my speech
How do I slow down

So I say the beginning, the middle and the end
Why can't I just download and transmit my
thoughts
It's hard at times to communicate, co-relate and
say it

I wish I was on a high-octane zoom
Where MAGIC turns me into a live wire...

Lost and found

I got tangled and lost
in my love story

Love took
And I gave
With all my heart, at first
Then over time
I didn't realise
How much it took
How hard it got
but unbeknown to me, it continued...

Magic Porridge pot
I was not
I got empty of my SELF

Tears, anger, rage
All weaved their own sad web
And it was a free fall

BREAKDOWN

Then, POSITIVITY and COURAGE
Stepped in
To help me take that first step

To understand, my LOSS
To regenerate my SELF
To inch away and find
underneath the layers of who I am

But with this loss, I FOUND
my precious and very own family
my life is richer for having them
And it is a delicate balance that
I must maintain
to give but not all
the me and the scattered parts of my heart within
each one of my dear ones

Loving, giving and losing ain't easy
It is so hard ....too damn much
But have to keep trying, learning and breathing
until I do

Stress

Face muscles Tense
Forehead Frowns inch deep; refuses to budge
Smile LOST
Mouth Straight
The whole body DRAINED
Of all Energy
Thoughts whirling constantly
Head Muddled
Heart Fizzled
Of all hope and pride
BREAK POINT
Tears follow in a release
Deep breaths
F-O-R-G-E-T
Breathe in LOVE
Breathe out all STRESS
Let it go
Erase
Make way for fresh new happy memories

Lowly dredges

When does a soul start to cheat?
When does it become weak?
When does it break its integrity?
Without integrity is there any humanity?

When does debasement start?
With that first step or
Slowly...
It creeps on with every ill deed
Until all humanity/ goodness is gone

Instead what's left is a shell
Full of the most depraved soul

A soul that is weak
So, it lies to self and others
It lives in a bubble of fantasy
Oh, so afraid
To go within miles of reality
The reality makes them feel
INCAPABLE
Of laughter, courage or love
EMPTY
FRUSTRATED

Unable to find a way out of their LIE
Ever...
It lives forever in hell
Tortured by the ill deeds done

Trying to understand why did they
go wrong that first time, with that little step
that grew each time
and in the end, took away Everything

Awakening

This is the year of awakening
Of learning about my self
And its relationships with me and others

How it's strong, fearless and amazing
Having faith in myself
On the relationships, that help
And hurt...

When we focus too much
On relationship with others
It almost, always leads us astray

To bring us back on track
Have to refocus and nurture
Our relationship with ME

What's our path in this realm
gets clearer with each test
That comes in shape of
Difficult relationships

They temper our soul
To rise above the surface and touch
To reflect on others' choices

To encourage and listen
To Grow

Patience and listening
to heart and intuition
Is the key
To look within
and find the endless answers
From our soul that's learnt so much from its
previous lifetimes

You may get sucked in, may deviate
But then you need to concentrate
And remember...
the relationship with I
Be content, be clear
Leave your legacy for your nears and dears

Crossroads

How often in life we come to one?
And then there's a choice that must be made

I always took the longer one
The one that made me experience
Laugh, sing, cry and rage and feel with all my
sensations

What I have come to learn is this
These crossroads help me be who I am
I choose the path
And then I face whatever demons or gods await
I use all that I have known
And what is unknown helps me grow

And that's why I chose to come
To grow and experience - diplomacy and
patience
Things that are hard to balance with- honesty
and spontaneity

My mum learnt a bit and then she passed it on
For me to learn and fathom and strike the
delicate balance
Once I do, to move on and progress on other
things that interest me

Mama

Mama I cried
Mama I tried
Wishing she was here

To have her back in my life
But she is gone forever
And I am here alone
Lost a bit

The love is lost
Or is it?
The emptiness and loneliness
Seems endless and scary
But doesn't have to be

The love remains
Inside
Her thoughts remain
Inside
Inside our head
Inside our heart

Just accept
The physical world
And it's limitations

And tap into
Your world within
That knows...

The memories
Of love
Of caring
Of tenderness and laughter
Of her warm, loving hugs
Of thoughtfulness and kindness

Of mum...

Death

An ending or a new beginning?
Always life and then a death
A baby is born and an old life ends...

It's time to grow up
Start a new chapter
To remember
And to cherish the memories
Of the life passed

Time to heal
With a flood of tears
Emptiness, and loneliness
In crowds

How do you carry on?
Why must you carry on?
When do you know it's time to stop
And let them go in the next realm

When your own time comes u know
You say goodbyes and go
Can't stay, must disconnect
From all the loving chords and say bye bye

But when it isn't
you must stay
And face the lonely emptiness
slowly each day
Until you learn to accept
That your purpose
is not the same perhaps
So, you will know
when your time is up
Not just yet!

Happy

Bubbles, giggles, laughter

Lots of jumping, hopping, skipping

Exploring heart, sharing thoughts,

Games, jokes, fun

Togetherness

Tenderness

Gentleness

Humour

Compliments

Kindness

Thoughtfulness

Lots of love

Need more days like this...

Tandem flying

We went on a tandem paraglide

It was so cool

Like a bird in the sky

Larking about and having fun up so high

I loved the view

AMAZING

My heart, so happy, enjoying

Ecstatic

Majestic

Maybe I will fly again someday

All together in the sky

Flying in my rocket with aliens and me

Flying in my rocket with aliens and me
Who wanted to go to the seaside
To see the beach
And have a treat
Of fish and chips and ice cream

We flew to Brighton
And saw the pier
Bounced on the trampoline
And had lots of fun and cheer

Then came back to Burgess Hill
For a roast dinner and peas
Then had a pudding of ice cream, if you, please

Then we were all tired and ready for bed
So we flew back in our rocket
To alien land
We said goodbye until next time
When I will take them to the zoo.....
10,9,8,7,6,5,4,3,2,1,0.........

Experiment lab

My favourite place
On this planet
Where I concoct my
Inventions to amaze

The pile of poo
Smelly goo
Are too good to be true
Yucky and smelly
Any boy aged 7's
Dream come true

The best one of all
Which is too exciting
And will guarantee to enthral
All boys big and small
Is the one to make
A giant, scary dinosaur

First I need
Is a handful of clay
Then I mould it
To make it stay
Dry and cool air it needs
To make the body of my Mr. Mean

Flying saucer

Flying saucer I dream of you
Every night I wish where are you?

I want to fly high up in space
To a dream of an alien land far far away.
Will you come to my dream tonight?
And take me on a magical flight?

Is there any space to go to the loo?
And is there a kitchen to make cake too?

So, let's get started on our voyage
To travel up millions of miles in space
To meet new aliens and make lots of friends
In this new land of creatures fierce
Let's get started, I will close my eyes
And count 1,2,3......

Vroom, vanish, I am off...
Flying over the sea
The snow and the mountains are all left far
behind
I am zooming up at supersonic speed
And when I wake up, our adventure will keep
me happy

I love you flying saucer as much as you do me